How to sail your own Ship

Zandra Mae Cochrane

How to sail your own ship

Written by: Zandra Mae Cochrane

ISBN: 978-1-7644630-5-8

Copyright © 2024
All rights reserved. No part of this book may be reproduced, stored in a retrieval system, or transmitted in any form or by any means, electronic, mechanical, photocopying, recording, or otherwise, without the prior written permission of the copyright owner.

First Edition: December 2024
Published in Australia

Table of Contents

Chapter 1: Launching for voyage

Chapter 2: Sailing through Life Storms

Chapter 3: Forming Alliances

Chapter 4: Conquering aspirations

Chapter 5: Diving into Adventures

Chapter 6: Personal Growth

Chapter 7: Reflecting on the Journey

Chapter 8: Your Own Ship, Your Own Rules

My Dearest Alhan,

As I sit down to write this book, my heart swells with love and pride for the incredible person you are becoming. I want to share with you the reasons behind writing this book and the deep love and lessons it carries within its pages.

This book is a labor of love, inspired by my own journey as an international student in Australia. When I first set foot in tthis distant land, I was filled with dreams and aspirations, but also faced with countless challenges. Balancing my studies with working five different part-time jobs was no easy feat. There were days when exhaustion seemed overwhelming, and moments when I questioned my own strength. But through it all, I learned invaluable lessons that shaped me into the person I am today.

I wrote this book for you, my dear Alhan, because I want to share those lessons with you. Life is a vast ocean, and each of us must learn to navigate its waters. This book is a guide to help you steer through the storms and find your own path. It is a testament to the resilience, determination, and courage that I discovered within myself here in Australia.

I want you to know that no matter where life takes you, you have the strength to overcome any obstacle. This book is a reminder that you are never alone on your journey. It is filled with stories of perseverance, hard work, and the importance of never giving up on your dreams. I hope it serves as a beacon of light, guiding you through the darkest of times and helping you find your way.

Remember, my dear Alhan, that you are capable of achieving greatness. Embrace the challenges, learn from them, and always believe in yourself. This book is my gift to you, a piece of my heart and soul, and a testament to the unbreakable bond we share.

With all my love,

Your Mom

Chapter 1
Launching for Voyage

As you prepare to launch your voyage, remember that your journey is uniquely yours. Much like a ship setting sail on the open sea, you have a destination in mind and a course to navigate. Your **values**, **passions**, and **dreams** are your compass, guiding you through the vast and unpredictable waters of life. Embrace your individuality and be confident in your choices, for they will lead you to places only you can reach.

Confidence is your anchor in the face of uncertainty. Trust in your abilities and the decisions you make, even when the seas are rough. It is through these challenges that you will grow and discover your true potential. Each wave you ride and each storm you weather contribute to your personal growth and discovery. Celebrate the uniqueness of your journey and respect the paths that others take, for it is in this diversity that we find strength and inspiration.

Embarking on your personal journey is an exciting step, akin to setting sail on the vast and unpredictable ocean. Each of us has a unique path in life, and recognizing this individuality is crucial as we navigate through various experiences and challenges. This chapter, "**Launching for Voyage**," is dedicated to understanding and embracing your unique journey and the confidence needed to steer your own ship.

Just as every ship has its own course to navigate, every person's life journey is distinct. Your inner compass—formed by your values, passions, and dreams—guides you through this journey. Embracing your individuality means acknowledging and celebrating what makes you unique. It involves trusting your instincts and setting your own course, rather than conforming to the expectations of others. Your individuality is your greatest asset, and it will lead you to places only you can go.

When I first moved to Australia last June 2023 as an international student, I faced numerous challenges that tested my resolve and confidence. Balancing my studies with working five different part-time jobs was incredibly demanding. I remember my first job was a cleaner at the same time a gardener and there were moments of doubt and exhaustion, but I had to trust my instincts and stay true to my goals. This period in my life taught me the importance of embracing my unique journey. I learned that my path, with all its struggles and triumphs, was uniquely mine and that I needed to navigate it with confidence.

Confidence is crucial when embarking on your voyage. Just like a captain confidently steers their ship, you must trust your judgment and be willing to take risks. Being confident in your choices means believing in your abilities and decisions, even when faced with uncertainty. Confidence empowers you to make bold moves and pursue your goals with determination. Remember, it's your journey, and only you can decide the best route to take.

Throughout my journey in Perth, Western Australia, I had to make choices that were not always understood or supported by others. By being confident in my decisions and embracing the lessons learned from each experience, I was able to grow and achieve my objectives. I remembered I've travelled six hours away from the city, Geraldton, a regional area, and have worked as a general manager, just to embark a new journey of believing my confidence. This personal story serves as a powerful example of how embracing individuality and being confident in one's choices can lead to personal growth and fulfillment.

The vast ocean is unpredictable, much like life itself. Embracing uncertainty involves being open to new experiences and understanding that not everything will go according to plan. Each wave and storm you encounter are opportunities for growth and learning. By embracing the unknown, you build resilience and adaptability, essential traits for navigating through life's challenges. It's the unexpected twists and turns that often lead to the most rewarding destinations.

The journey itself is as important as the destination. Along the way, you will discover more about yourself—your strengths, passions, and even your limitations. Each experience, whether it's a success or a setback, contributes to your personal growth. This continuous process of self-discovery enriches your life and helps you become the best version of yourself. Embrace each moment of learning and growth as a vital part of your voyage.

Respecting Others' Journeys

Just as no two ships sail the same route, no two individuals have the same life journey. It's important to respect and celebrate the paths that others take. This fosters a supportive and diverse community where everyone's unique journey is valued. By recognizing that there is no single "right" way to live, you encourage a culture of acceptance and understanding. Your path is yours alone, but it's enriched by the relationships and connections you build along the way.

While studying, I was fortunate to meet a diverse group of friends, all international students like myself. Each of us came from different backgrounds, with unique stories and dreams. We were united by our shared experience of studying abroad, but each of us faced our own set of challenges. Some of my friends were working late-night shifts at shopping stores, Zyra, Christine and Gerlyn, while others, Kyle, took up cleaning jobs early in the morning. There were also those who worked in restaurants and cafes, Jay, balancing their shifts with demanding coursework.

We often gathered to share our experiences, providing support and encouragement to one another. Those friends of mine have worked three jobs while pursuing their degree & passion. Despite their hectic schedule, they always found time to check in on me and offer a helping hand. Their perseverance was inspiring and reminded me all of the strength that lies in determination.

Our diverse journeys taught us the value of empathy and understanding. We respected each other's struggles and celebrated each other's victories, no matter how small they seemed. These interactions enriched our lives and fostered a sense of community that made the difficult times more bearable. Respecting others' journeys not only strengthened our bonds but also broadened our perspectives, teaching us that there is no single right way to navigate life.

Through these friendships, I learned that supporting one another and appreciating each person's unique path is crucial. Our different experiences and backgrounds became our collective strength, helping us to overcome the challenges we faced as international students juggling various responsibilities.

This lesson in respect and empathy is something I wish to pass on. Embrace the uniqueness of your journey, and always remember to value and support the diverse paths of those around you. Your relationships and connections will not only enrich your life but also help you sail through the storms with greater resilience and understanding.

Setting sail on your personal journey isn't just about charting a course through the seas but about self-development along the way. Each wave you navigate and each storm you weather contribute to your personal advancement. The sea, like life, is full of challenges and opportunities for self-improvement.

Every obstacle you overcome is a lesson in personal evolution. Your journey is a continuous process of growth and development, much like a sailor who gains confidence with every successful voyage. Embrace each experience as a step towards individual progress and personal transformation.

Remember, the **open sea offers endless possibilities for enhancing oneself**. With every mile you sail, you will find opportunities for self-enhancement that will leave you enriched with new skills and greater wisdom. This is the essence of your journey - **to sail through life, growing and evolving with every wave you meet.**

"The journey of a thousand miles begins with one step."
— Lao Tzu —

- What are some of your unique qualities that you are proud of?

- What short-term goals can you set for yourself to start your journey?

- How do you feel about stepping out of your comfort zone?

Chapter 2
Sailing through Life Storms

My journey as an international student in Perth, Western Australia was akin to navigating through a tumultuous sea, each wave representing a new challenge. The decision to leave my family, kids, homeland and pursue education in a foreign country was both exhilarating and daunting. Without the comfort of my family here, Ben, I faced the profound loneliness that often accompanies such a significant life change. I thank him for putting a lot of love and commitment to that kind of surreal responsibility to my life. The sense of isolation was heightened by the need to juggle multiple part-time jobs to support my children and family back home. This responsibility weighed heavily on my shoulders, adding another layer of complexity to my already challenging life.

One of the most formidable challenges was managing my time effectively. Balancing demanding academic responsibilities with five part-time jobs required meticulous planning and prioritization. I created a detailed schedule that allocated specific hours for studying, working, and self-care. This discipline allowed me to meet my academic deadlines while ensuring that I could provide for my family financially. Each job presented its own unique set of challenges, from long hours and physical exhaustion to the emotional toll of being away from my loved ones. However, I persevered because I understood the importance of my role as both a student and a provider. To combat the overwhelming sense of loneliness, I sought solace in the company of fellow international students who were experiencing similar struggles. Building a support network was crucial; it provided a sense of community and belonging that mitigated the feelings of isolation. We shared our stories, celebrated our small victories, and provided emotional support during tough times. This camaraderie was a lifeline, reminding me that I was not alone in my journey.

Resilience was the cornerstone of my ability to navigate through these storms. I learned to view each setback as an opportunity for growth rather than a roadblock. When faced with adversity, I adopted a problem-solving mindset. Breaking down large problems into smaller, manageable tasks made them less intimidating and more approachable. For example, when I struggled to balance work and studies, I re-evaluated my schedule and prioritized tasks based on urgency and importance. This systematic approach to problem-solving allowed me to stay focused and productive.

Maintaining a **positive mindset** was essential. There were days when the weight of my responsibilities felt unbearable, but I found strength in focusing on the progress I had made and the goals I was working towards. Practicing gratitude helped shift my perspective from what was lacking to what was achievable. I celebrated small successes, like completing a difficult assignment or receiving positive feedback at work. These moments of positivity acted as beacons of light, guiding me through the darkest times.

Practical advice for anyone facing similar challenges begins with the importance of time management. Creating a structured schedule and sticking to it can significantly reduce the chaos that comes with juggling multiple responsibilities. Building a support network is equally vital; having a community of people who understand and share your experiences can provide invaluable emotional support. Developing resilience is key; embrace each challenge as a learning opportunity and focus on finding solutions rather than dwelling on problems.

Finally, maintaining a positive outlook is crucial. **Surround yourself with positivity,** whether it's through supportive friends, engaging in hobbies you love, or simply taking a moment each day to reflect on what you're grateful for. These practices can help sustain your spirit and keep you motivated through the toughest times.

My journey as an international student in Australia was fraught with challenges, but it was also a period of immense personal growth and development. By managing my time effectively, seeking support, maintaining a positive mindset, and honing my problem-solving skills, I was able to overcome the obstacles I faced. My experiences taught me the importance of resilience and the power of a positive outlook no matter what.

For anyone facing similar challenges, my advice is to stay focused on your goals, seek support when needed, and view each challenge as an opportunity to learn and grow.

Remember, every storm you sail through makes you a stronger and more capable navigator of your own ship.

Resilience, my dear Alhan, is the ability to bounce back from setbacks and keep moving forward. It's about viewing each challenge as an opportunity to learn and grow. Remember, every storm you face in life is temporary, and with determination and a positive outlook, you can navigate through it. Embrace the lessons that come your way, for they will shape you into a stronger and more capable individual.

I want you to know that no matter what storms you encounter, you have the strength within you to sail through them. Stay positive, seek support, and face each challenge with courage. Your unique journey is filled with endless possibilities, and I am confident that you will navigate it with grace and resilience. **Always remember, you are the captain of your own ship, and you have the power to steer it towards your dreams.**

"The greatest glory in living lies not in never falling, but in rising every time we fall."
— Nelson Mandela —

- Describe a recent challenge you faced and how you overcame it.

- How do you handle stress and difficult situations? What strategies work best for you?

- Reflect on a time when you supported a friend during their tough times. How did it make you feel?

Life, much like a voyage, is best experienced when shared with others. Friendships and relationships are the wind that fills your sails, propelling you forward even when the seas are rough. They provide support, guidance, and companionship, making the journey more enjoyable and less daunting. I quickly learned the invaluable role that friendships and relationship play in navigating life's challenges.

Far from home and family, I found solace in the company of Ben, his family, his friends, Katherine & Matt together with their children, Nate & Vann, who owned a piece of paradise here in Chittering. It is filled with a beauty of spectacular nature. I always sit down facing the mountainous view from afar which seems to be endless. It felt like home, where I can rest and away from anxiety and worriness here on earth. Their home, surrounded by beautiful scenery, felt like a serene escape from the pressures of daily life. Katherine's cooking was nothing short of extraordinary—each dish she prepared was a delightful reminder of home, filled with flavors that brought comfort and joy. Her culinary skills and warm hospitality made every meal feel like a special occasion. Matt's welcoming nature and the playful energy of Nate and Vann added to the charm of their household, creating an environment that was both nurturing and joyous.

Adding to this people, were Adam and Echo, a lovely couple and friends of Ben, who provided a home filled with warmth and encouragement; Echo, a strong mother, inspired me with her resilience, while Adam's supportive nature reminded me of Ben's generosity.Their home was a place of warmth and comfort, much like Ben's.

Another memorable encounter was meeting Tennel and John, who brought a burst of energy and fun into my life. Tennel, with her lively and energetic personality, was a whirlwind of positivity and enthusiasm. Her vibrant spirit was infectious, making every moment spent with her full of laughter and joy. At first, I must admit, I was a bit hesitant due to my naturally shy personality. However, Tennel's welcoming nature and genuine warmth quickly put me at ease. John complemented her perfectly with his calm and steady demeanor, providing a balanced dynamic that made their company truly enjoyable.

Being welcomed into their circle of friends made me feel embraced by a larger community, one that extended beyond immediate family. Their friendship helped me come out of my shell and embrace new social experiences with more confidence.

I found also myself with fellow students whom I became friends, Zyra, Christine, Gerlyn, Jay, & Kyle who were on similar journeys, each facing their own set of hurdles. I have also witnessed the profound concern I had to pray for my classmates who are struggling with their visa, Roldan, a father whose wife & kid is away but have shown a warrior in the battle of unknown. Omar, who shows the essence & meaning of a helping hand. Tracy & Kuya Robert, who shows that it may be hard to conquer those things unseen, but will be worth to defeat than to make yourself at weak.

Another remarkable friend I met was Zyra, whose boundless energy and fun-loving nature brought a sense of lightness to my life. Always ready with a smile and a listening ear, Zyra was someone I could rely on during tough times. Her generosity shone through when she lent me money, enabling me to send support back to my children when I was running out of funds. She continually reminded me to enjoy life and not be consumed by worries. Zyra's moral lessons and encouragement helped me stay positive, even when the road seemed rough. Despite her occasional childlike demeanor, which only added to her charm, her wisdom and kindness provided the support I needed. Her presence was a constant reminder that amidst life's challenges, there's always room for joy and compassion.

Christine was like a sister to me during the most challenging times of my life in Australia. She was always there to listen and offered me a place to stay in her apartment when everything seemed tough and hopeless. One vivid memory I have is of us going to St. Mary's Church in Perth, standing in line for free food. A woman confronted us, telling us we weren't allowed there, which was embarrassing, yet we managed to fill the moment with laughter and joy. Filling us well our stomach. Christine's survival skills were incredible; she always knew how to navigate difficult situations and find solutions, whether it involved money matters or simpler problems. Her support was unwavering, and she always found ways to help me see the light, even in the darkest times. I remember staying at her apartment for a week, feeling enveloped in her comforting presence, which helped chase away the darkness and brought a sense of hope back into my life. Her friendship was a beacon of light, providing the strength and resilience needed to keep moving forward.

Gerlyn, a hardworking mother who worked as a packer at Harvey Beef alongside her husband and child, Enon, became one of my strongest pillars of support. Her dedication to her work and family was truly inspiring. Gerlyn was one of my rocks; she always listened to my worries and helped me out whenever I needed it. There were times when I owed her money in order to support you my dear Alhan, and when your little brother was sent to hospital for check up, but she never hesitated to lend a helping hand, understanding the struggles of being a mother and a sister. Her empathy and unwavering support were invaluable, providing me with the strength and reassurance needed to face the challenges of my journey. Gerlyn's friendship was a testament to the power of solidarity and mutual understanding, and I am forever grateful for her kindness and generosity.

Jay was one of those friends who, at first glance, seemed quiet and reserved. However, once you got to know him, you quickly realized that he had a fantastic sense of humor and a knack for making people laugh so hard that they forgot their problems, even if just for a moment. His jokes and playful nature were a constant source of joy and relief amidst the daily struggles. Jay reminded me a lot of my brother, James, who also had the unique ability to find humor in life's challenges and never forgot to laugh, no matter how tough things got. Jay's presence was a reminder that even in the face of adversity, laughter and a light-hearted perspective could be incredibly powerful tools for coping and staying resilient. His friendship brought much-needed levity and a sense of camaraderie that I will always cherish.

Kyle, the youngest among my friends, was always eager to explore life with a childlike curiosity. His personality was vibrant and refreshing, often reminding me of a newbie excited to experience everything for the first time. Despite his youthful exuberance, Kyle was always open and showed genuine concern for those around him. His willingness to listen and offer support was deeply appreciated. Though he sometimes canceled gatherings, it was always understandable given his busy schedule and the unpredictability of youthful endeavors. Kyle's enthusiasm and caring nature made him a delightful presence, adding a touch of youthful energy and joy to my journey.

I feel incredibly fortunate and grateful for having met such wonderful friends and their boundless energy and unwavering support, even lending me any form of help when I was in need, brought light and positivity into my life.

This is one of the most significant friendships I formed whom we all met at Illoura College with Ms. Fiona, she's the best teacher who has the ability to turn criticism into possitivity and wisdom. She shared invaluable moral lessons whcih for me have extended far beyond the classroom. Her dedication to her work and her students was truly inspiring. She always encouraged me to see constructive criticism as a tool for growth, helping me develop resilience and a positive mindset. Ms. Fiona's unwavering commitment to education and her genuine care for her students made her an extraordinary mentor. Her lessons and guidance have left a lasting impression on me, shaping my approach to challenges and personal growth. Her influence is something I will always carry with me, reminding me of the power of dedication and the importance of lifelong learning We immediately connected over our shared experiences of juggling multiple jobs while striving to excel academically.

They all worked multiple part-time jobs to support their studies and family back home. I thought I was battling alone but despite their hectic schedule, they always had a smile on their face and a word of encouragement for everyone around. Their positive attitudes were infectious, and their friendship became a source of strength for me.

Throughout my journey here in Australia, I was also blessed with the support of some incredibly kind and generous Filipinas, whose warmth and compassion made all the difference. Ate Marigrace, Christine, Jean, Nelyn, and Jara opened their hearts and homes to me, allowing me to clean their houses in exchange for delicious, comforting meals & money that reminded me of home. Their laughter and friendship turned what could have been a lonely, difficult time into one filled with joy and camaraderie. Then there was JC, whose empathy knew no bounds. When I found myself without a place to stay, JC welcomed me into his home without hesitation, offering me a roof over my head and a safe space to call my own. The kindness and support of these wonderful individuals were a beacon of light in my life, helping me stay strong and focused on my goals. Their generosity and love are something I will always cherish and hold close to my heart.

Adding to this circle of support was Ivan, a fellow Filipino from my hometown. Ivan became my confidant and listening ear, providing comfort and understanding when I needed it most. His presence was a constant reminder of home and the strength of where I am. The kindness and support of these wonderful individuals were a beacon of light in my life, helping me stay strong and focused on my goals. Their generosity and love are something I will always cherish and hold close to my heart.

Before I forgot I'd like to share you this, one of the most memorable experiences during my time in Australia was being invited to a formal lunch by a wonderful family, Ben's family. It was the first time in my life that I had been invited to such an elegant setting somwhere in Swan View. The restaurant was beautifully set up, and the sight of the forks and knives neatly arranged on the dining table was both new and intimidating. My nerves were calmed by the welcoming smiles and comforting assurance of the family that everything would be okay.

Erin, has an angelic face, very lovely and kind-hearted sister of Ben, was the one who extended the invitation and pick us up. Her warmth and friendliness put me at ease immediately. Then I met Helen, Ben;s mom, a very warm and motherly figure who reminded me so much of mom, Miramar. Her presence was incredibly comforting and filled the void of missing my family back home. Steve, Ben's dad, with his gentle demeanor, reminded me of dad,Jimmy, making me feel like I was in the company of family.

I was also introduced to Josh, and Nick with his partner, who were full of energy and kindness. Their enthusiasm and curiosity about my culture made the lunch even more enjoyable. Kate, another member of the family, was accompanied by her partner, who is also a teacher. Their presence reminded me of the universal nature of teaching and how it connects people from all walks of life. Ben's 90-year-old grandmother was another beacon of warmth and hospitality. She called me over for a chat, making me feel incredibly welcome with her wisdom and stories. Her grace and kindness were a testament to the welcoming nature of the community. Ben's aunt and uncle were equally accommodating, always ready to offer support and make me feel at home. Their generosity and love are something I will always cherish and hold close to my heart.

Despite my initial fear of using the unfamiliar utensils, the family's smiles and reassurances made me feel at home. This experience not only broadened my understanding of different dining customs but also strengthened my resolve to embrace new experiences and cultures. Their kindness and hospitality left a lasting impact on me, showing me the importance of extending a helping hand and making others feel welcome. It was a beautiful reminder that, no matter where we are in the world, the bonds we form with others can bring us comfort and joy. Their generosity and love are something I will always cherish and hold close to my heart.

Through all of them, I realized the importance of choosing the right people to share your journey with. It's essential to surround yourself with individuals who uplift you, share your values, and support your dreams. Building strong, supportive connections begins with being open and honest about your own struggles and aspirations. Vulnerability fosters trust and deeper connections. We often shared our challenges and successes, which helped us build a bond of mutual respect and understanding.

To form meaningful alliances, it's crucial to actively listen to others, offer help when needed, and celebrate their achievements as if they were your own. These moments of collective joy strengthened our connections and reinforced the importance of mutual support.

Here are some practical tips I have learned and acquire for building strong, supportive relationships:

- **Be Genuine**: Authenticity attracts genuine people. Be yourself and allow others to see the real you. This fosters trust and deeper connections.

- **Active Listening**: Pay attention to what others are saying without planning your response. Show that you care by listening attentively and empathetically.

- **Be Supportive**: Offer help when your friends and loved ones are in need and celebrate their successes. Support creates a foundation of trust and loyalty.

- **Vulnerability**: Don't be afraid to share your struggles and ask for help. Vulnerability can deepen relationships and foster mutual support.

- **Choose Wisely**: Surround yourself with positive, like-minded individuals who share your values and aspirations. The right people will uplift and inspire you.

- **Communicate Openly:** Open and honest communication prevents misunderstandings and helps resolve conflicts quickly, strengthening the relationship.

Friendships and relationships are vital to navigating life's journey. They provide the support and companionship needed to face challenges and celebrate successes. Just as my relationships with them enriched my life and helped me overcome obstacles, you too can build strong alliances by being genuine, listening actively, and supporting those around you.

Remember, the people you choose to share your journey with can make all the difference, helping you sail smoothly through life's storms and toward your dreams. By forming meaningful connections, you enrich your voyage and create lasting bonds that will carry you through any adversity.

"A friend is one who knows you and loves you just the same."
— Elbert Hubbard —

- Who are the people in your life that support you the most? How do they help you?

- What qualities do you value most in a friend or partner?

- Reflect on a time when you formed a new friendship. What made it special?

Chapter 4

Conquering, Aspirations

Charting your course in life is much like setting sail on a long voyage. It requires careful planning, determination, and the willingness to adjust your sails when the winds change. Goal setting is a crucial part of this journey, as it provides direction and purpose. When I first arrived in Perth, Australia as an international student, my dream was to obtain a degree while supporting my kids & family back home. This aspiration seemed daunting at times, but by setting clear, actionable goals, I was able to navigate through the challenges and achieve my dreams.

The first step in goal setting is to define both short-term and long-term goals. Short-term goals are like the stepping stones that lead you to your ultimate destination. They should be specific, measurable, achievable, relevant, and time-bound (SMART). Thanks to Ms. Fiona, she nailed this abbreviations to my course. For example, during my studies, a short-term goal I set for myself was to complete all my assignments a week before their deadlines. This allowed me to manage my time effectively and reduce stress.

Long-term goals, on the other hand, are your ultimate aspirations. These goals require a broader vision and a strategic plan. For me, the long-term goal was to graduate and secure a stable job in my field of passion which is Teaching. To achieve this, I broke down my long-term goal into smaller, manageable tasks. I prioritized my studies, sought works at schools as a relief Education assistant, and networked with professionals in my industry. Each short-term goal I accomplished brought me one step closer to my long-term aspirations.

Staying focused and motivated is essential in the pursuit of your goals. There were times when the workload was overwhelming, and balancing multiple part-time jobs added to the stress. However, I learned to visualize my success regularly. I imagined the day I would walk across the stage at graduation or receiving an email from immigration that my skilled visa was granted, which kept me motivated. Tracking my progress also helped me stay on course. I recorded my achievements, no matter how small, and used them as reminders of how far I had come.

Surrounding yourself with supportive individuals is another critical aspect of achieving your goals. My friends, who were also international students, and Ben became my support system here. We encouraged each other, shared study tips, and celebrated our successes together. Having a network of people who believe in you and your dreams can provide the motivation and encouragement needed to keep going, even when the journey gets tough.

Here are some practical steps that I have learned and acquired to help you chart your course and conquer your aspirations:

- **Define Your Goals:** Clearly articulate what you want to achieve. Write down your goals and ensure they are SMART.

- **Break Down Goals:** Divide your long-term goals into smaller, manageable short-term goals. This makes the process less overwhelming and more achievable.

- **Create an Action Plan**: Develop a step-by-step plan outlining the actions needed to reach each goal. Include deadlines to keep yourself accountable.

- **Stay Focused:** Regularly review your goals and progress. Adjust your plan as needed to stay on track.

- **Seek Support:** Surround yourself with supportive individuals who encourage and motivate you. Mentors, friends, and family can provide valuable guidance and accountability.

- **Stay Motivated:** Celebrate your achievements, no matter how small. Recognize your progress and use it as fuel to keep moving forward.

- **Overcome Obstacles:** Anticipate challenges and develop strategies to overcome them. Stay resilient and adaptable in the face of setbacks.

Charting your course through goal setting and taking actionable steps is essential for conquering your aspirations. By setting both short-term and long-term goals, creating a detailed action plan, and staying focused and motivated, you can navigate the journey toward your dreams with confidence and determination.

Remember, the journey may be challenging, but with perseverance and the right mindset, you can sail your own ship to success.

"Life is either a daring adventure or nothing at all."
— Helen Keller —

- What new hobby or skill would you like to explore? Why?

- Describe a time when trying something new led to personal growth.

- How do you stay motivated to learn and grow? What inspires you?

Chapter 5
Diving into Adventures

Exploring new waters is about stepping out of your comfort zone and embracing the unknown with courage and curiosity. This willingness to take risks can lead to significant personal growth and open doors to exciting opportunities. When I first moved to Perth, Australia as an international student, I faced the challenge of adapting to a new culture, balancing my studies with multiple part-time jobs, and being miles away from family, including you. Each of these experiences pushed me far beyond my comfort zone, but they also led to incredible growth and opportunities that I might never have encountered otherwise.

One of the most significant risks I took was accepting a part-time job as a cleaner in a field completely unrelated to my studies. This job required me to interact with a diverse range of people, manage tasks I had no prior experience with, and work in a fast-paced environment. Initially, I felt overwhelmed and questioned my decision, but I soon realized that this experience was teaching me invaluable skills such as effective communication, time management, and adaptability. These skills not only helped me excel in my job but also proved beneficial in my academic pursuits and future career.

Another instance of stepping out of my comfort zone was joining an online community group focused on motivation and dedication to wok. As someone who had never been involved in community activities, this was a significant leap. However, this decision exposed me to new perspectives, allowed me to contribute to meaningful projects, and helped me build a network of like-minded individuals. This experience broadened my horizons and taught me the importance of community engagement and responsibility.

Traveling within Australia also provided numerous opportunities for personal growth. During my day offs, I made it a point to explore different suburbs of the country. These trips were not just vacations; they were adventures that pushed me to navigate unfamiliar terrains, interact with locals, and immerse myself in diverse cultures. One memorable trip was to the Albany with Ben and Harvey with my circle of Disney friends, where I took up pictures despite my initial fear of the ocean. This adventure was transformative, as it helped me overcome my fear and allowed me to experience the breathtaking beauty of the world.

Through these experiences, I learned that taking risks and exploring new waters are essential for personal growth. Stepping out of your comfort zone allows you to discover new interests, develop new skills, and build resilience. Each risk you take is an opportunity to learn and grow, even if the outcome is not what you initially expected. The key is to approach these adventures with an open mind and a willingness to embrace the unknown.

Here are some practical tips that I have learned for stepping out of your comfort zone and exploring new waters:

- **Start Small:** Begin with manageable risks, such as trying a new hobby or taking a different route to work. Small steps can build your confidence and prepare you for larger challenges.

- **Set Goals**: Identify specific areas where you want to grow and set goals to push yourself beyond your comfort zone. This could be learning a new language, joining a club, or traveling to a new destination.

- **Stay Curious**: Cultivate a mindset of curiosity. Approach new experiences with an eagerness to learn and discover, rather than focusing on potential failures.

- **Embrace Failure**: Understand that not every risk will lead to success, and that's okay. Failure is a valuable teacher that provides insights and opportunities for growth.
- **Seek Support:** Surround yourself with supportive individuals who encourage you to take risks and try new things. Their encouragement can provide the motivation needed to step out of your comfort zone.
- **Reflect on Experiences:** After taking a risk, take time to reflect on the experience. What did you learn? How did it help you grow? This reflection can reinforce the value of stepping out of your comfort zone.

Exploring new waters by stepping out of your comfort zone and taking risks is a vital part of personal growth. My experiences here taught me the importance of embracing the unknown and seeking new adventures. Each risk I took, contributed to my growth and opened up new opportunities. By following the tips provided and maintaining an adventurous spirit, you too can navigate the vast ocean of life and discover the incredible potential within you.

Remember, the most rewarding journeys often begin with a single step into the unknown.

"Life can only be understood backwards; but it must be lived forwards."
— Soren Kierkegaard —

- What are the three most important lessons you've learned so far in your journey?

- How have your experiences shaped who you are today?

- What are your goals for the future, and how do you plan to achieve them?

In the journey of life, learning and growing are akin to diving into uncharted waters—exciting, sometimes challenging, but always enriching. Continuous learning and self-improvement are essential to navigating this journey successfully. As an international student in Australia here, I experienced firsthand the importance of embracing every opportunity to learn and grow. Away from family and familiar surroundings, I faced the challenge of balancing rigorous academic requirements with multiple part-time jobs to support you and our family back home. This chapter, "Diving into Adventures," emphasizes the importance of lifelong learning and personal development and offers practical advice on how to cultivate new skills, hobbies, and passions.

One of the most significant lessons I learned during this time was the value of setting aside time for self-improvement, despite the pressures of daily life. For instance, I dedicated a few hours each week to learn new skills that would enhance my career prospects. I enrolled in online courses to improve my proficiency in various software tools, like Canva, which later proved invaluable in my academic and professional pursuits. By continuously seeking knowledge, I was able to stay competitive and open new doors of opportunity.

Exploring new hobbies also played a crucial role in my personal growth. Amidst the hustle and bustle of my busy schedule, I discovered a passion for cooking. Experimenting with new recipes not only provided a creative outlet but also served as a stress-reliever. Each culinary adventure taught me the importance of patience, precision, and creativity—skills that translated well into other areas of my life. This new hobby enriched my life which I never ever felt before, giving me a sense of accomplishment and joy outside my academic and work responsibilities.

The importance of seeking out new experiences cannot be overstated. My time here in Australia, I took every opportunity to travel and immerse myself in different cultures. Each trip, whether it was a weekend getaway to a nearby town, Chittering, or a day off to explore the Albany, broadened my perspective and fostered personal growth. These adventures pushed me out of my comfort zone, teaching me resilience and adaptability. They helped me develop a deeper understanding of myself and the world around me, making me more open-minded and empathetic.

In addition to personal pursuits, formal education and professional development played a significant role in my journey of continuous learning. Attending workshops, participating in seminars, and enrolling in additional courses provided me with valuable knowledge and skills that were directly applicable to my career. Staying updated with industry trends and advancements ensured that I remained competitive and capable in my field.

Cultivating a growth mindset is fundamental to continuous learning and self-improvement. This involves viewing challenges as opportunities for growth rather than obstacles. There were times when managing multiple responsibilities felt overwhelming, but I chose to see these challenges as chances to build my resilience and problem-solving abilities. By adopting this mindset, I remained open to new learning experiences and persevered in the face of difficulties.

For you, Alhan Farisha, embracing the adventure of learning and growing means actively seeking out opportunities to enrich your life. Set aside time to develop new skills, whether through online courses, books, or workshops. Explore new hobbies that ignite your passion and provide a sense of fulfillment. Seek out new experiences that push you beyond your comfort zone and broaden your horizons.

Remember, each new skill you acquire, every hobby you pursue, and every adventure you embark on contributes to your personal growth and self-improvement.

"Personal growth is not a matter of learning new information but of unlearning old limits." — Alan Cohen

- What personal goals have you set for yourself in the past year? How have you worked towards achieving them?

- Describe a moment when you stepped out of your comfort zone and how it contributed to your personal growth.

- Reflect on a challenge you faced recently. What did you learn from it, and how did it help you grow as a person?

As we sail through life's vast and unpredictable ocean, it's essential to pause and reflect on the lessons we've learned along the way. Each experience, challenge, and victory shapes us, making us more resilient, wise, and empathetic. My journey here, far from the comfort of family and familiar surroundings, I faced numerous challenges that tested my resolve and strength. These experiences provided invaluable lessons that have profoundly shaped who I am today.

One of the most significant lessons I learned is the power of resilience. The road to achieving my dreams was filled with obstacles, from balancing demanding academic work with multiple part-time jobs to dealing with the emotional strain of being away from my family, including you, my dear Alhan. There were times when the weight of these responsibilities felt overwhelming. However, I discovered that resilience is not about never falling but about having the strength to get back up each time you do. Each setback was a lesson in perseverance and determination, teaching me that challenges, no matter how intimidating, can be overcome with grit and tenacity.

Self-awareness emerged as another critical lesson. Being alone in a foreign land forced me to confront my fears, limitations, and aspirations. This period of introspection allowed me to understand my strengths and weaknesses better. I learned to leverage my strengths while acknowledging and working on my weaknesses. This self-awareness fostered personal growth, helping me make informed decisions and take responsibility for my actions. It taught me the importance of continuous self-improvement and the value of being true to oneself.

Gratitude also became a cornerstone of my journey. Amidst the struggles, I realized the importance of appreciating the small victories and the support I received from Ben, friends and mentors. Recognizing the positive aspects of my experiences, even in the face of adversity, shifted my perspective and enhanced my overall well-being. Gratitude helped me focus on what I had achieved and the kindness of those around me rather than dwelling on the hardships. This positive outlook fueled my motivation and provided the strength to keep moving forward.

Reflecting on these lessons, I encourage you, Alhan, to take time to look back on your own journey. Think about the challenges you've faced, the victories you've celebrated, and the people who have supported you. Reflect on how these experiences have shaped you and what you have learned from them. Keep a journal to document your thoughts and progress. My personal laptop became my journal here. This practice will help you stay grounded and motivated, serving as a reminder of your resilience and growth.

In your own journey, embrace each challenge as an opportunity for growth. Develop self-awareness by regularly evaluating your strengths and areas for improvement. Cultivate gratitude by recognizing and appreciating the positive aspects of your experiences.

Remember that every setback is a stepping stone toward success and that every lesson learned adds to your wisdom and strength.

"Reflecting on the Journey" is about understanding that every experience, whether good or bad, contributes to your personal development. The lessons of resilience, self-awareness, and gratitude have shaped me into who I am today, and they can do the same for you.

By reflecting on your journey, you gain insights that guide you forward, helping you navigate life's storms with confidence and purpose. Embrace these lessons, for they are the wind in your sails, propelling you towards your dreams and aspirations.

"Life can only be understood backwards; but it must be lived forwards."
— Soren Kierkegaard —

- What are the three most important lessons you've learned so far in your journey?

- How have your experiences shaped who you are today?

- What are your goals for the future, and how do you plan to achieve them?

As we come to the final chapter of this journey, "Your Own Ship, Your Own Rules," I want to reinforce a powerful message of independence and empowerment. Throughout your life, you will encounter various challenges, opportunities, and decisions that will shape your path. It's crucial to remember that you are the captain of your own ship. You have the power to navigate your own path and make decisions that align with your values and aspirations. My experiences here have taught me the significance of taking charge of my own destiny, and I want to share these lessons with you.

When I first arrived here, the sheer magnitude of being in a foreign country, miles away from family, and managing multiple responsibilities was overwhelming. However, I quickly realized that relying on my own strength and making my own decisions were essential to thriving in this new environment. One of the most significant decisions I made was to pursue something I desired and never expected to come in my life while working several part-time jobs to support you and our family back home. This decision required immense dedication and careful planning, but it was guided by my deep sense of responsibility and my desire to create a better future for us.

Taking control of my schedule was a pivotal step in asserting my independence. I crafted a detailed plan that balanced my commitments, work hours, and personal time. This allowed me to stay organized and focused, ensuring that I could meet my goals without becoming overwhelmed. Each decision I made, whether it was accepting a new job, choosing a study method, or managing finances, was driven by a clear understanding of my priorities and long-term objectives. This autonomy gave me the confidence to navigate through the uncertainties and pressures of my circumstances.

Another key aspect of my journey was learning to trust my instincts. There were moments when I faced criticism or doubt from others, but I remained steadfast in my choices. For instance, when I decided to take on an additional job to ensure we had enough funds for your education and well-being, some questioned my ability to handle the workload. However, I trusted my capacity to manage my time and energy effectively. This decision ultimately paid off, providing the financial stability we needed and reinforcing my belief in my own judgment.

Building a support network was also crucial in empowering myself. While it's important to make your own decisions, having a circle of trusted friends and mentors can provide valuable advice and encouragement. Ben and my friendships with other people, who were also navigating their unique paths, were a source of strength and inspiration. We supported each other, shared our experiences, and celebrated our successes. These relationships enriched my journey, reminding me that while I was steering my own ship, I was not alone in the ocean.

Embracing the mantra of "Your Own Ship, Your Own Rules" means acknowledging that you have the authority to set your own course. It's about understanding that your life is yours to navigate, and the choices you make should reflect your true self and aspirations. It involves taking responsibility for your actions, learning from your mistakes, and celebrating your achievements. This sense of empowerment is the foundation for living a fulfilling and self-determined life.

As you sail through life, remember that you hold the compass. Trust your instincts, make decisions that align with your values, and don't be afraid to carve out your own path, even if it deviates from the expectations of others. Your journey is uniquely yours, and you have the power to shape it according to your dreams and aspirations. By embracing your independence and taking charge of your destiny, you can navigate through life's challenges with confidence and purpose.

This final chapter, "Your Own Ship, Your Own Rules," is a testament to the power of independence and empowerment. My experiences here have shown me that taking control of your own life is crucial for achieving your goals and finding fulfillment. I encourage you to embrace this message as you navigate your own journey.

Remember that you are the captain of your ship, and you have the power to set your own rules and steer your course towards a bright and successful future.

"You are the master of your destiny. You can influence, direct and control your own environment. You can make your life what you want it to be."
— Napoleon Hill —

- What does independence mean to you? How do you practice it in your daily life?

- Describe a decision you made that significantly impacted your life. How did you come to that decision?

- Reflect on a time when you trusted your instincts. What was the outcome?

To My Dearest Kids, Family & Friends,

In every challenge you face and every dream you pursue, always remember that you are never alone. My love and support are with you in every step of your journey. You are incredibly strong, capable, and filled with endless potential. Trust in yourself and embrace the adventures life brings. Know that I believe in you, today and always.

With all my love,

Zandy

Positive Affirmations for you:

"I am strong, capable, and resilient."

"I believe in my dreams and have the power to achieve them."

"I embrace challenges as opportunities for growth."

"I am worthy of love, success, and happiness."

"I trust myself to navigate life's journey with confidence."

Zandra Mae is a dedicated teacher and a loving mother of two wonderful children, Alhan Farisha and Zach Eros Demetrius. Her journey as an educator has been marked by her unwavering commitment to nurturing young minds and inspiring them to reach their full potential. As a mother, Zandra's experiences have been enriched by the joys and challenges of raising her children, shaping her into a resilient and compassionate individual.

Living miles away from her family and navigating the complexities of life as an international student, Zandra found solace and strength in her passion for writing. Her book, "How to Sail Your Own Ship," is a heartfelt reflection of her journey and the invaluable lessons she has learned along the way. Inspired by the love for her children and her desire to share her wisdom, Zandra's writing is a testament to the power of determination, courage, and the unwavering support of loved ones. Her story is a beacon of hope and encouragement for those who seek to navigate their own paths with confidence and grace.

"How to Sail Your Own Ship" is an empowering and inspirational guide which navigates the reader through the tumultuous seas of life, offering valuable lessons on independence, resilience, and personal growth. Drawing from the author's own experiences as an international student and the support from wonderful individuals she met along the way, Zandra provides practical advice, reflective journal prompts, and heartfelt anecdotes to inspire readers to take control of their destiny. The book emphasizes the importance of self-awareness, gratitude, and the courage to steer one's own course, making it a must-read for anyone seeking to embark on a journey of self-discovery and empowerment.

www.ingramcontent.com/pod-product-compliance
Lightning Source LLC
Chambersburg PA
CBHW040002110526
44587CB00001BA/30